Opening up Philippians

ROGER ELLSWORTH

DayOne

'Joy in jail through Jesus is the theme of Philippians. And Roger Ellsworth's study of this rich, Christ-centred book can produce Christ-centred joy in the heart of every believer. Laden with insightful quotes and penetrating practical application, Opening up Philippians is a Bible study tool which belongs on every Christian's bookshelf!'

Dr. Phil Robert
President, Midwestern Baptist Theological Seminary,
Kansas City, Missouri

'Some bible studies simplify the bible by dumbing it down. Other bible studies dig deep into the text while losing their readers in the whirlwind of academic trivia. But Roger Ellsworth has the unique gift of making the bible simple, while retaining its majesty and glory. This study of Philippians pulsates with the joy and gravity of the apostle Paul's letter. It is must-reading for pastors and church leaders seeking to know the mind of Christ as given to us in the book of Philippians'

Russell D. Moore
Dean, School of Theology and Senior Vice President for Academic Administration, The Southern Baptist Theological Seminary, Louisville, Kentucky

First printed 2004
Scripture quotations are from the NKJV, Thomas Nelson Publishers, 1983

ISBN 1 903087 64-3

9781903087640

British Library Cataloguing in Publication Data available

Published by Day One Publications
Ryelands Road, Leominster, HR6 8NZ
Telephone 01568 613 740 FAX 01568 611 473

email—sales@dayone.co.uk
web site—www.dayone.co.uk
North American—e-mail-sales@dayonebookstore.com
North American web site—www.dayonebookstore.com

Designed by Steve Devane and printed by CPD

The following pages are lovingly
dedicated to my grandson,
Daniel William Ellsworth

List of Bible abbreviations

THE OLD TESTAMENT

		1Chr.	1 Chronicles	Dan.	Daniel
		2 Chr.	2 Chronicles	Hosea	Hosea
Gen.	Genesis	Ezra	Ezra	Joel	Joel
Exod.	Exodus	Neh.	Nehemiah	Amos	Amos
Lev.	Leviticus	Esth.	Esther	Obad.	Obadiah
Num.	Numbers	Job.	Job	Jonah	Jonah
Deut.	Deuteronomy	Ps.	Psalms	Micah	Micah
Josh.	Joshua	Prov.	Proverbs	Nahum	Nahum
Judg.	Judges	Eccles.	Ecclesiastes	Hab.	Habakkuk
Ruth	Ruth	S.of.S.	Song of Solomon	Zeph.	Zephaniah
1 Sam.	1 Samuel	Isa.	Isaiah	Hag.	Haggai
2 Sam.	2 Samuel	Jer.	Jeremiah	Zech.	Zechariah
1 Kings	1 Kings	Lam.	Lamentations	Mal.	Malachi
2 Kings	2 Kings	Ezek.	Ezekiel		

THE NEW TESTAMENT

		Gal.	Galatians	Heb.	Hebrews
		Eph.	Ephesians	James	James
Matt.	Matthew	Phil.	Philippians	1 Peter	1 Peter
Mark	Mark	Col.	Colossians	2 Peter	2 Peter
Luke	Luke	1 Thes.	1 Thessalonians	1 John	1 John
John	John	2 Thes.	2 Thessalonians	2 John	2 John
Acts	Acts	1 Tim.	1 Timothy	3 John	3 John
Rom.	Romans	2 Tim.	2 Timothy	Jude	Jude
1 Cor.	1 Corinthians	Titus	Titus	Rev.	Revelation
2 Cor.	2 Corinthians	Philem.	Philemon		

Overview

The city of Philippi was located very importantly in the north east of Greece, and provided an excellent gateway for the gospel to be taken from Asia Minor into the continent of Europe. Philippi was named after Philip of Macedon who had taken control of the settlement around 300 BC. In 168 BC, it was annexed by the Romans. Other battles followed over the next century or so, and the city gained particular prominence in 31 BC when, after the battle of Actium, it gained possession of the 'Italic right'. This meant that the colony (as it now was) enjoyed exactly the same rights as the Romans of Italy themselves did.

This Roman outpost proved to be a place of strategic importance for the apostle Paul in bringing the gospel of the grace of God to a much wider audience.

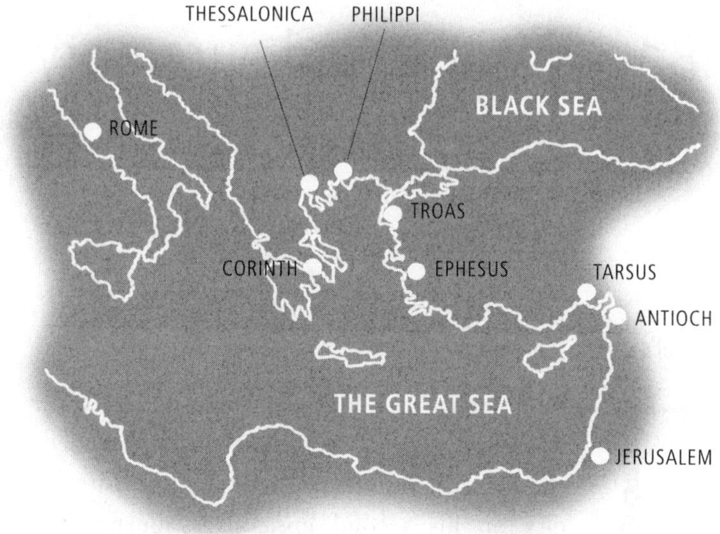
THESSALONICA
PHILIPPI
BLACK SEA
ROME
TROAS
CORINTH
EPHESUS
TARSUS
ANTIOCH
THE GREAT SEA
JERUSALEM

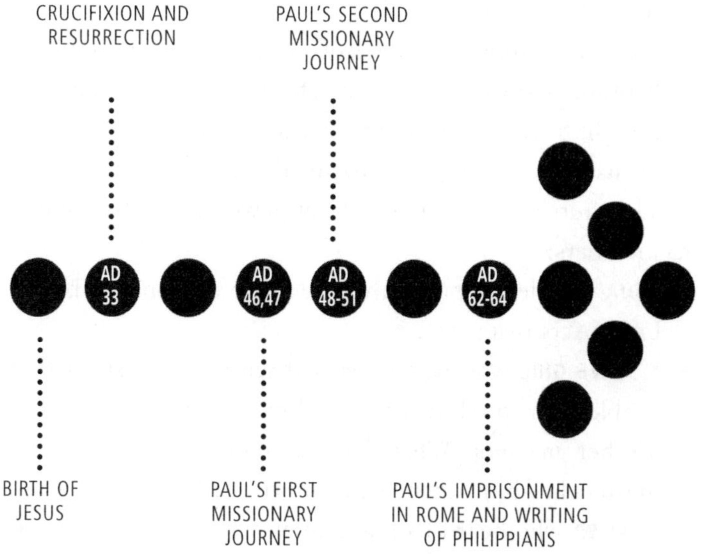
CRUCIFIXION AND RESURRECTION
PAUL'S SECOND MISSIONARY JOURNEY
AD 33
AD 46,47
AD 48-51
AD 62-64
BIRTH OF JESUS
PAUL'S FIRST MISSIONARY JOURNEY
PAUL'S IMPRISONMENT IN ROME AND WRITING OF PHILIPPIANS

Background and summary

Paul's visit to Philippi

The letter to the Philippians was written by the apostle Paul to the church that he had founded in the Macedonian city of Philippi. Paul visited this city on his second missionary journey after receiving a remarkable vision in which 'a man of Macedonia' pleaded with him: 'Come over to Macedonia and help us' (Acts 16:9).

Luke, the author of the book of Acts, describes the response of Paul and his missionary team to the vision: '… immediately we sought to go to Macedonia, concluding that the Lord had called us to preach the gospel to them' (Acts 16:10).

The church Paul started in Philippi would number among its members:

- **LYDIA**, a seller of purple, whose heart was opened by the Lord (Acts 16:11–15);
- **A SLAVE GIRL** who was possessed with an evil spirit that enabled her to tell fortunes and make a handsome living for her masters. When Paul cast out her demon, her masters had him arrested and imprisoned (Acts 16:16–24);
- **A JAILER** who heard Paul and Silas sing praises to God at midnight. After a mighty earthquake opened the prison,

> this man, wrongly assuming he had lost all his prisoners, was about to take his life. But hearing Paul's assurance that all were still there, and being under great conviction by the Spirit of God, the jailer cried out: 'Sirs, what must I do to be saved?' (Acts 16:30). The missionaries immediately responded: 'Believe on the Lord Jesus Christ, and you will be saved…' (Acts 16:31).

Paul and Silas' visit to Philippi came to a hasty end when the city officials learned that they were Roman citizens. This meant that the officials had acted illegally in having them beaten and imprisoned without a trial. Fearing legal trouble of their own, the magistrates prevailed upon Paul and Silas to leave town (Acts 16:35–40).

Paul's letter

Paul's visit to Philippi was in A.D. 51. Approximately eleven or twelve years later, Paul picked up his pen to write the believers there. His letter is the second of his 'prison epistles', that is, letters he wrote while he was incarcerated. (Ephesians is the first of these. Colossians and Philemon are the others.)

The place of Paul's imprisonment was Rome. It seems likely that this was not the Roman imprisonment which ended in his execution (2 Tim. 4:6–8).

The apostle's reasons for writing are as follows:

(1) to report on his circumstances;

(2) to express appreciation for their concern for him and a gift they had sent to him by Epaphroditus;

(3) to assure them that Epaphroditus, who became ill while with Paul, had ministered satisfactorily to him and was now well enough to return to them;

(4) to urge them to fulfil various duties;

(5) to warn them about the ever-present danger of false teachers.[1]

To use an analogy from mining, in the ore of all these practical details, we find a bright, glittering vein of irrepressible joy. The apostle Paul was in the midst of very trying circumstances, but those circumstances did not, and could not, diminish his abounding joy.

Again and again in this brief letter he uses the words 'joy' and 'rejoice.' He writes: '… I rejoice, yes, and will rejoice' (1:18). He also says: 'Finally, my brethren, rejoice in the Lord' (3:1). And he adds: 'Rejoice in the Lord always. Again I will say rejoice' (4:4).

As we read this letter we immediately get the strong impression that Paul is not writing to tell the Philippians how to have joy. He rather writes for the purposes stated above. But as he deals with these matters, the joy keeps bubbling up and spilling over.

This should, in fact, be the case with all the children of God. While we are engaged here and there, whether with mundane, humdrum matters or with pressing and urgent responsibilities, those around us should be able to detect a joy that is fed from the hidden spring of life in Christ.

There can be no doubt that Christ was the source of the apostle's joy. His letter to the Philippians contains 104 verses. In those verses, we find some form of the name of Christ or a pronoun referring to Christ a total of sixty-one times.

Another of Paul's emphases is the mind. He uses such words as 'mind,' 'minds', 'minded,' and 'think' a total of eleven times in this letter.

When we put all these things together we arrive at this truth: Christian joy comes through having a Christ-centred mind.

Multitudes are obsessed with happiness and frustrated because they cannot find it. Why is this the case? Is this not the problem: we search for happiness instead of the thing that creates happiness?

I get the impression that Paul did not seek happiness. He sought to live for the Lord, and happiness found him. We need to learn that happiness is a by-product and it comes to us as we occupy ourselves with serving the Lord.

With these things in mind, we set sail on the sea of Philippians. Our study will require us to look at the various themes with which the apostle deals. But it will also require us to maintain a constant look-out for the recurring theme of joy as it bubbles to the surface.

For further study ▶

FOR FURTHER STUDY

1. Read Acts 17:1–18:22. What other cities did Paul visit on his second missionary journey? What notable experiences did he have?
2. How many times do the words 'joy' and 'rejoice' appear in Philippians?

TO THINK ABOUT AND DISCUSS

1. What are some situations that modern Christians encounter which make it difficult to rejoice?
2. Paul was occupied with the Lord while he was in prison. How can we occupy ourselves with God?
3. The church at Philippi was composed of a range of widely differing people, all of whom were in relationship with Christ. Does your church reflect such a range of differences? Can you see opportunities for your church to demonstrate that, despite the differences of its members, you are all in fellowship with one another because of your relationship with the Head?

1 Paul introduces his letter

(1:1–11)

Paul's relationship with the church at Philippi was a good one and the tone of his letter to them expresses the warmth of his love and the depth of their fellowship in the gospel

Paul greets the church (vv. 1–2)

Timothy, Paul's son in the ministry, was with Paul at the time of this writing, and is, therefore, included in the greeting. There was no need for Paul, as was his custom, to identify himself as an apostle. There was no debate about this in the church of Philippi. The people there gladly acknowledged Paul's apostleship and the authority this entailed. Paul was content, therefore, to refer to himself and to Timothy as 'servants of Jesus Christ' (v. 1).

We might be inclined to feel sorry for Paul. A life of servanthood! What a depressing thought! But the truth is we are all servants throughout our lives. We are either servants of the devil or servants of the Lord. The service of Satan is hard and oppressive, but the service of the Lord brings joy and peace.

Paul addresses his letter to 'the saints in Christ Jesus who are in Philippi, with the bishops and deacons' (v. 1).

The word 'saints' means 'set apart.' All Christians are saints. God in grace has set them apart from people in general and made them his own special people for his own special purposes.

The 'bishops' refers to the pastors of the church, those who were responsible to watch over the church. The 'deacons' were those who had been selected to serve the church by giving attention to practical matters so the pastors could give their time to the Word of God and prayer (see Acts 6:1–7).

To all of these Paul extends his wish for 'grace' and 'peace' from God the Father and the Lord Jesus Christ. Grace is, of course, the spring or fountain from which all of God's blessings flow, and peace is one of the greatest of those blessings. Because believers have peace with God, they also have the peace of God, that is, a deep and abiding sense of peace within.

Paul gives thanks for the church (vv. 3–8)

For their fellowship from the first day (vv. 3–5)

Paul could not think of the Philippians without giving thanks to God for their fellowship in the gospel. The word 'fellowship' refers to sharing or holding something in common. We have a tendency to use the word very loosely these days. Any gathering of Christians in which there is a feeling of happiness and camaraderie is called 'fellowship'. We have almost made the word synonymous with good food and a few laughs. But that, of course, makes Christian fellowship no different from what unbelievers often enjoy.

We can be sure that the apostle had something far different—and better!—in mind. It was more than merely enjoying each other's company. It was partnership.

Christian fellowship is a marvel. People who by nature have nothing in common find a common life in Christ. Think again of Paul's ministry in Philippi. Lydia the slave girl and the jailer had nothing in common until they came to Christ (Acts 16). But the gospel of Christ made them partakers of the same life and partners in the same cause.

Christian fellowship is a marvel. People who by nature have nothing in common find a common life in Christ

Because of this bond of fellowship the Philippians had supported Paul in both his ministry and his imprisonment. They had done the former by sending gifts to him while he was in Thessalonica (4:14–16) and in Corinth (2 Cor. 11:9). They had done the latter by sending one of their number, Epaphroditus, to minister to Paul (2:25; 4:18).

The bond of fellowship between the Philippians and Paul was so very strong that he earnestly yearned to be separated from them no longer (v. 8). To remove all doubt from their minds about how very strongly he loved them he writes: 'I long for you all with the affection of Jesus Christ' (v. 8).

Paul could go no higher than this. His love for the Philippians was such that it reflected the love of Christ himself.

For their victory in the last day (v. 6)

As the apostle gave thanks for the Philippians' participation in the work of the gospel, he could not help but add a word of thanksgiving for the work of the gospel in them. He was thankful '… that he who has begun a good work in you will complete it until the day of Jesus Christ…'

Paul was very good at slipping little nuggets of breathtakingly glorious truth into the mundane portions of his letters. This verse is one of those nuggets. It tells us the following:

- **SALVATION IS GOD'S WORK.** The Philippians did not begin the work of salvation in themselves only to have God come along and add a little to it. It was entirely his work. God provided the way of salvation through his Son, Jesus Christ, and he even enabled the Philippians to receive that salvation.
- **SALVATION IS A GOOD WORK.** Salvation lifts the sinner from eternal condemnation and ruin and makes that person part of God's family and a partaker of God's eternal glory. Who would dare say that this is not a good thing?
- **SALVATION IS A SURE WORK.** God does not begin it and then abandon it somewhere along the way. He does not pull his people from the flames of destruction only to allow them to slip back and be consumed. God completes the work of salvation. We know what it is to plan a work and undertake a work only to see it fail. But it is not so with God. We must not picture him looking over the redeemed

multitude in eternity and saying: 'We did fairly well. Eighty per cent of the saved finally made it home.' God will not have to say such a thing because all his people will make it home. Not one will be missing! The faithful God will faithfully complete his work!

Paul prays for the church (vv. 9–11)

As the apostle began expressing his gratitude for the Philippians, he mentioned remembering them with joy in his prayers (v. 4). He then proceeded to share four requests that he had been offering on their behalf.

That their love would abound (v. 9)

This may seem to us to be a very strange request in the light of what we have already noted, that is, that the Philippian church was already characterized by love. We can be sure that Paul is not now denying what he has already stated. He is rather affirming that love is a grace in which we can always advance. No matter how much we love, we can love more.

> No matter how much we love, we can love more

He is also praying for them to abound in a certain type of love, that is, love with knowledge and discernment. He will soon find it necessary to warn them about the ever-present danger of false teachers (3:2,18–19). The Philippians would make themselves easy prey for such teachers if, in the interest of being loving, they were uncritically to accept everything that these teachers were presenting.

We should be keenly aware of this danger. How often the

church today has refused to stand against doctrinal error because someone argued that we must be loving! And, of course, love was understood to mean being agreeable and tolerant.

No one believed more firmly in love than Paul, and yet he did not hesitate to rebuke a fellow apostle for compromising the truth (Gal. 2:11–21). Paul did this because he understood that love and truth are not enemies. The most loving thing we can do is stand for the truth in a loving way.

That they would approve the things that are excellent (v. 10)

The word 'approve' means to 'distinguish'. The idea of seeing through to the heart of a matter is involved. Paul is praying that his readers would be able, in the midst of competing issues and concerns, to see what is truly important and deserving of priority, and that they would be able to make wise spiritual decisions.

That they would be sincere and without offence (v. 10)

The word 'sincere' translates a word that originally meant 'pure' or 'unmixed'. In ancient times merchants would often patch cracked porcelain with wax. A merchant who wanted his customers to be assured of his integrity would advertise his porcelain as 'without wax'.[1]

Paul's desire for the Philippians was that they be 'without wax', pure and blameless in their conduct, so they could stand unashamedly before their Lord. Paul constantly lived with that day on which he would stand before Christ in view, and he wanted his readers to do the same. The key to living this day is to remember that great forthcoming day.

That they would be filled with the fruits of righteousness (v. 11)

William Hendriksen writes: 'Paul prays that in the hearts and lives of the Philippians there may be a rich spiritual harvest, consisting of a multitude of the fairest fruits of heaven; such as, love, joy peace, longsuffering, kindness, goodness, faithfulness, gentleness, self-control (Gal. 5:22–23), and the works which result from these dispositions.'[2]

As Paul reflected on the fruits of righteousness, he undoubtedly called to mind the words the Lord Jesus spoke to his disciples on the night before his crucifixion: 'I am the vine, you are the branches. He who abides in me, and I in him, bears much fruit; for without me you can do nothing' (John 15:5).

It is not surprising, therefore, that Paul reminds his readers that the fruits of righteousness 'are by Jesus Christ.' And because they are produced by Christ, they are 'to the glory and praise of God' because Jesus did all for the glory of God (John 8:29; 15:8; 17:1,4).

For further study ▶

FOR FURTHER STUDY

1. The apostle Paul identified salvation as God's good work (1:6). Read Ephesians 1:3–14. When did God begin this work? What aspects of this work can you identify?
2. Paul also described salvation as a sure work that will not fail. What makes it so sure? Read John 10:27–30; Romans 8:31–39; 1 Peter 1:3–5.

TO THINK ABOUT AND DISCUSS

1. In what ways can you help to promote fellowship in your church and with other Christian friends?
2. Paul prayed that the Philippians would abound in love. Read 1 Corinthians 13 and suggest three or more ways in which Christian love may be clearly demonstrated in your circumstances.

2 Paul rejoices in his imprisonment

(1:12–26)

It is easy for us to understand Paul giving thanks for the Philippians. Every Christian prizes his brothers and sisters in Christ. However, it is much harder for us to understand Paul giving thanks for his imprisonment and that is precisely what we find him doing in these verses

As Paul was imprisoned in Rome, it is very likely that he was chained twenty-four hours per day to a Roman guard, each guard on a shift lasting several hours. He could enjoy no privacy as long as these circumstances endured. How could he possibly give thanks in the midst of such difficulty? We will never understand this until we understand how Paul loved the gospel of Jesus Christ. He was a gospel-centred and gospel-impassioned man. We have heard of people looking through rose-colored glasses. Paul wore Christ-coloured glasses. He could write: 'For to me, to live is Christ...' (v. 21).

Wearing his Christ-coloured glasses, the apostle tells the

Philippians why he was rejoicing over his imprisonment: '... the things which happened to me have actually turned out for the furtherance of the gospel...' (v. 12).

His words demand that we take a long and hard look at ourselves. What does the gospel mean to us? Does it mean enough that we are willing to suffer hardship in order for it to prosper? Or do we put our own comfort and ease above the gospel?

As we look at Paul's rejoicing over his imprisonment, we see him giving emphasis to two major themes: the good that he could see and the good that he expected to see.

The good that Paul could see (vv. 12–18)

In these verses the apostle describes how his imprisonment had been used by God for the furtherance of the gospel.

Contact with unbelievers (v. 13)

Finding himself constantly under guard, the apostle Paul immediately realized that he had been given a marvellous opportunity for sharing the gospel. He began letting his guards and others know that he was in chains because of Christ. This would have undoubtedly caused the guards to seek an explanation, and Paul was ever eager and ready to share the full message of Christ.

We may also assume that the way in which Paul conducted himself had a profound effect on those guards. Having come to embrace the Christ whom Paul preached, the guards themselves began sharing their faith with those around them. The gospel succeeded so admirably in this way that Paul was able to include these words in the conclusion of this letter:

'All the saints greet you, but especially those who are of Caesar's household' (4:22).

Paul's example teaches us to view every situation in which we find ourselves as an opportunity for spreading the gospel. With this in mind, the Christian can, for example, see a hospital bed as a pulpit and the hospital as a mission field.

No Christian can instil faith in other hearts—that is the work of God. But wherever a believer goes, he should leave a favourable impression of his Christianity with those with whom he or she has associated.

Motivation for fellow-preachers (vv. 14–18)

In these verses Paul talks about two groups of his fellow-preachers: those who were preaching with a feeling of envy toward him and those who were preaching with good will for him (v. 15).

THOSE PREACHING OUT OF ENVY

William Hendriksen explains the first group in this way:

> It should be borne in mind that there was a church in Rome long before Paul arrived there. It can scarcely be doubted, therefore, that certain preachers in Rome had attained a degree of prominence among the brothers. With the arrival of Paul and especially with the spreading of his fame throughout the city ... it is easy to understand that these leaders were beginning to lose some of their former prestige. *Their* names were no longer mentioned so often. Hence, they became envious of Paul. Their motives in preaching Christ were not pure or unmixed.[1]

These men evidently saw the imprisonment of Paul as their opportunity to come to the forefront again. They went about their preaching, therefore, with renewed vigour and zeal.

In candidly speaking of these preachers, Paul was shining a floodlight on a shameful reality of his day. Sadly enough, it has persisted through the ages and continues today. It is the reality of rivalry and ambition among preachers and this reality exists because preachers are not as good as the message they preach. Afraid that a fellow-minister will become known as a better preacher, they force out of their minds what the Bible says about the cursedness of pride and the need for humility.

While Paul refuses to justify the envy of these men, he does take delight in the fact that they are vigorously preaching Christ. What a man this Paul is, even willing for others to speak ill of him if they would also speak well of Christ!

THOSE PREACHING OUT OF GOOD WILL

These were preachers who admired Paul, and, learning about his faithful stand for Christ even in prison, were enflamed with zeal for preaching Christ in their own situations.

The situation in which Paul found himself was not good. Imprisonment deprived him of the opportunity to pursue his ministry in the way that he would have chosen and it separated him from many dear friends. But God brought good out of it, and Paul rejoiced in that. As Paul pondered his circumstances, he may very well have found himself thinking about the testimony of Joseph. Years after being sold by his brothers into slavery, Joseph was able to say to them: 'But as for you, you meant evil against me; but God meant it for good, in order to bring it about as it is this day, to save many people alive' (Gen. 50:20).

We cannot always trace the hand of God, but we can always trust the heart of God. His heart is devoted to working all things together for good for his people (Rom. 8:28).

The good that Paul expected to see (vv. 19–26)

While Paul rejoices in the good that his imprisonment has accomplished, he looks forward with eager expectation to being released soon. He writes: '… I know that I shall remain and continue with you all for your progress and joy in the faith, that your rejoicing for me may be more abundant in Jesus Christ by my coming to you' (vv. 25–26).

While Paul is optimistic about being released, he realizes that he has not been given a special revelation from God concerning this matter. It is possible that he will not be released but will rather be executed.

Paul did not tremble at the thought of death. He considered it to be a most welcome prospect. He expressed a desire 'to depart and be with Christ' which would be for Paul 'far better' (v. 23).

Such words seem very strange to many people these days. This life is generally regarded as being so very wonderful that we must cling to it at all costs. We would have no trouble agreeing with Paul if he had said, 'I would prefer to die than to continue in prison.'

We are all familiar with situations that are so dreadful that death is a relief. But Paul is not saying that death is better than the worst of life. He is saying death is better than the best of life. In other words, he was not longing for death as the way out of unbearable circumstances. He was longing for it as the way into unspeakably glorious circumstances.

We can be sure that Paul would have readily agreed with these lines:

> Lord, it belongs not to my care
> Whether I die or live;
> To love and serve Thee is my share,
> And this thy grace must give.
>
> If life be long, I will be glad,
> That I may long obey;
> If short—then why should I be sad
> To soar to endless day?[2]

This is not some sort of blind idealism or heroic optimism on Paul's part. It is all rooted in Jesus Christ. Why would Paul not desire to be with Christ? It was the Lord Jesus Christ who had delivered him from the kingdom of Satan and from eternal ruin; it was Christ who had sustained him through his trials and afflictions; it was Christ who promised him eternal life without the possibility of trials and afflictions.

If we cannot share Paul's desire, it is because we have not seen as clearly as he has the wonder of what Christ has done.

Verse 21 constitutes a powerful test for us all. Put a blank after the phrase 'to live is' and another blank after the phrase 'and to die is'. How would you fill in the blanks? If you say 'to live is money', you must say 'to die is to leave it all behind'. If you say 'to live is fame', you must say 'to die is to be forgotten'. If you say 'to live is pleasure', you must say 'to die is to lose it all'. But if you can join Paul in saying 'to live is Christ', you can also join him in saying 'to die is gain'.

The puritan Richard Sibbes understood Paul's yearning to be with Christ. He wrote:

> Why should we then fear death, that is but a passage to Christ? It is but a grim sergeant that lets us into a glorious palace, that strikes off our bolts, that takes off our rags, that we may be clothed with better robes, that ends all our misery, and is the beginning of all our happiness. Why should we therefore be afraid of death, it is but a departure to a better condition.[3]

We usually associate being torn between options with being unhappy. Paul is a torn man, but he is also a vibrantly happy man. He is torn because, on one hand, he wants to continue his ministry, and, on the other hand, he wants to be with Christ. But he is a joyful man because he knows he will not be the loser in either case. If he dies, it will be for the cause of Christ and will bring honour to his name. If he is released, it will be so he can continue to promote the cause of Christ. In either case, Christ will be magnified (v.20), and Paul, the Christ-centred man, will be deliriously happy.

If all we care about is Christ, we are happy with whatever Christ decides.

For further study ▶

FOR FURTHER STUDY

1. Paul had a heart of concern for unbelievers. Read Romans 9:1–3 for insight into the depth of his concern. Read Matthew 9:36–38. How was Jesus affected by the sight of the multitudes? What did he teach his disciples on this occasion?
2. How could Paul regard death as better than life in this world? Read 1 Corinthians 15:20–58; 2 Corinthians 5:1–8; 1 Thessalonians 4:13–18.

TO THINK ABOUT AND DISCUSS

1. It is easy to quote Romans 8:28 unthinkingly. Mention one or two incidents where you have seen the outworking of the truth of this verse.
2. You have learned that a dear friend or family member has been diagnosed with a terminal illness. How does Paul's teaching here help you to give practical advice to that person? How does it help you, personally, to prepare for death?

3 Urgent appeals

(1:27–2:11)

Paul has given thanks for the Philippians and shared his prayer for them. He has also shared with them his reasons for rejoicing in his imprisonment. Now he calls them to discharge important duties

Concerning the faith of the gospel (1:27–30)

He has celebrated their fellowship in the gospel; he has rejoiced in the furtherance of the gospel; now he calls them to join him in contending for the faith of the gospel (v. 27).

What is the faith of the gospel? It is the truth of the gospel. Paul's exhortation, then, is the same as the one Jude issued to his readers when he urged them to 'contend earnestly for the faith which was once for all delivered to the saints' (Jude 3).

Many would have us believe that the gospel is so ambiguous and nebulous that no one can speak with certainty about it. They would have us believe that it is one thing to one person and something quite different to another and no one can say who is right and wrong.

It seems that we love precision in every area of life. We want the surgeon to be precise; we don't want him just to be 'in the neighbourhood' when he opens us up to remove a tumour. We want precision in sports; we don't want the referee to signal a touchdown when the ball carrier is still ten yards away from the goal line. We want precision in our banking; we don't want our bank to short-change us by a few hundred dollars or pounds.

> But when it comes to the truth of God, our love for precision seems to disappear

But when it comes to the truth of God, our love for precision seems to disappear. The reason is not hard to identify. If the gospel cannot be defined, we are absolved of responsibility. We are off the hook!

While we comfort ourselves with the thought of an imprecise gospel, the Bible insists on the opposite. The gospel is the good news of the precise details of what God has done in the redeeming work of Jesus Christ. It is the message of the holy God providing in Christ the righteousness that sinners must have in order to stand acceptably in the presence of God. It is the message of God propitiating or appeasing his wrath against sinners by pouring out that wrath upon the Lord Jesus Christ.

It's not hard to see why so many find this gospel objectionable. It assumes our sin and our meeting a holy God. It speaks of the reality of God's wrath. It insists on the finality of Jesus Christ.

Standing fast as soldiers (v. 27)

This gospel has always been assaulted and attacked and continues to be to this day. Because it was being attacked in his time, Paul urged the Philippians to 'stand fast in one spirit ... for the faith of the gospel.'

With these words Paul calls his readers to unite around the faith of the gospel as soldiers and athletes. The Philippians would have immediately understood the words 'stand fast.' They would have thought of the phalanx in which the army was able to withstand the advance of the enemy because each soldier stayed in his place and did his job. Warren Wiersbe pointedly writes: 'The Christian life is not a playground; it is a battleground. We are *sons* in the family, enjoying the *fellowship* of the Gospel (Phil. 1:11); we are *servants* sharing in the *furtherance* of the Gospel (Phil. 1:12–26); but we are also *soldiers* defending the *faith* of the Gospel'.[1]

Christians must resist Satan's attacks on the truth of the gospel by refusing to break rank and flee the battlefield.

Striving together as athletes (v. 27)

With the words 'striving together' Paul takes his readers from the realm of military endeavour to that of athletic endeavour. His emphasis is still on unity. The athlete is not to compete for himself alone but for the good of the team.

Paul's point is clear. Soldiers and athletes cannot succeed apart from when they are united. They have to be characterized by one mind and one spirit as they work to achieve a single objective and so it must be with the church.

Standing and striving without fear (vv. 28–30)

Christians are not to live in fear of their adversaries, powerful as they may be. Why are we not to give way to fear? Paul gives the following reasons:

- the opposition of our adversaries is temporary. Their opposition to Christians constitutes opposition to God, and that opposition will finally end in perdition or destruction (2 Thess. 1:6–10).
- the opposition of our adversaries proves our salvation. Matthew Henry notes that believers have been given two 'precious gifts.'[2] One is to believe in Christ. The second is to suffer for Christ. The fact that our adversaries cause us to experience the second gift indicates that we have truly received the first. While suffering is never pleasant, it is a privilege and honour to suffer for the Christ who suffered so very much to save his people.

While suffering is never pleasant, it is a privilege and honour to suffer for the Christ who suffered so very much to save his people

Concerning the unity of the church (2:1–11)

In these verses the apostle moves away from the church's work of standing for the truth of the gospel in a hostile world to call for unity between believers within the life of the church.

The incentives for unity (vv. 1–2)

THEIR EXPERIENCE OF CHRIST (V. 1)

Paul here piles one phrase on top of another, each beginning with 'if'. William Hendriksen notes: 'Paul says "If", not as if he doubts whether the condition is really true, but simply to emphasize that when the condition is present, the conclusion should also be present.'[3]

Was it true, then, that they had found consolation in Christ and comfort in his love? Had they indeed found fellowship with Christ himself through the work of the Holy Spirit? Had they truly found affection and mercy from Christ? They could not, then, fail to reflect the reality of these things in their relationships with one another. If, as Hendriksen observes, the condition is present, so should the conclusion be.

THE JOY OF THE MINISTER (V. 2)

Paul writes: '... fulfil my joy by being like-minded, having the same love, being of one accord, of one mind.'

As we have noted, the apostle is already a joyful man even in the midst of distressing circumstances. But he knows his joy could be even greater. It is, we might say, almost to the brim. It could reach the brim and overflow if the Philippians would only heed his appeal for unity.

Christians owe a great debt to those who have laboured diligently to bring them to Christ and to bring them up in the truths of Christ. One of the best ways to show gratitude for such leaders is by avoiding dissension. Only his own experience of the saving work of Christ brings the spiritual leader more joy than the unity of those he has been called to lead.

The essential ingredients of unity (vv. 3–11)

THE INGREDIENTS ARE CLEARLY STATED (VV. 3–4)

What is necessary for unity within the church? Paul leaves no doubt at all about this. It requires the Philippian believers to humble themselves and to put the concerns of others above their own concerns.

Could anything be more at odds with modern dogma which constantly tells us to put ourselves first? This notion has so affected (or infected!) the church that Jesus' teaching that one is to love his neighbour as himself (Matt. 22:39) is now construed to mean that we must first learn to love ourselves before we can love our neighbours.

Paul's formula for joy stands out in Philippians. It is J (Jesus) O (Others) Y (Yourself). So very often we try to have Paul's joy while we reverse his formula. It cannot be done. We can't spell joy by putting the Y first, and we can't find joy by putting ourselves first.

THE INGREDIENTS ARE POWERFULLY ILLUSTRATED (VV. 5–11)

Nothing cuts across the grain of human nature quite so much as being called to humility and putting others first. Being fully aware of this, Paul is not content merely to assert these things but rather drives his teaching home with undeniable proof.

Paul didn't have to look far for this kind of proof. It was readily available in the example of the Lord Jesus Christ.

In these verses he takes us through three stages of our Lord's experience and to the very heart of redemption. He sets forth his purpose in doing so with these words: 'Let this mind be in you which was also in Christ Jesus' (v 5).

The Philippians are again to focus their attention on Christ, not out of mere academic or theoretical interest, but with a view to emulating his example.

The first stage is Christ's glory before coming to this world. Paul puts it succinctly by telling us that he, Christ, was in the form ('morphe') of God and equal with God (v. 6).

The second stage is Christ's humility in coming. Paul says Christ '… made himself of no reputation, taking the form of a bondservant, and coming in the likeness of men. And being found in appearance as a man, he humbled himself and became obedient to the point of death, even the death of the cross' (vv. 7–8).

We should not be able to read these words without a sense of awe and wonder stealing over our hearts. If anyone ever had the right to insist on his rights, it was the Lord Jesus. But his concern for others (those whom the Father had given him) was such that he refused to insist on his rights. He did not cling to his divine prerogatives, but willingly laid aside all the trappings of his glory and took our humanity.

It is crucial for us to understand that in doing this he did not cease to be God. God cannot cease to be God! He rather laid aside the glories and riches of heaven and 'the independent exercise of authority'[4] and added our humanity to his deity so he was at one and the same time fully God and fully man.

It would have been an act of stupendous humility if the Lord Jesus had done nothing more than take to himself our humanity. But he did much, much more. In that humanity, he died. Dying itself would have been astonishing humility, but there is even more: his death was like no other. It was 'the death of the cross.'

Of course, Jesus was not the only man who died on a cross. Many did. But no other death on a cross compared to his: there he became the sin-bearer for his people, standing in their place and receiving the wrath of God instead of them. The death of Christ was nothing less than Christ experiencing hell for his people so they would never have to experience that hell themselves.

Who can measure the gap between the throne and the cross? And who can plumb the depths of the love behind the cross, the love of God for sinners? Charles Wesley celebrates this love in these lines:

> 'Tis mystery all! The immortal dies!
> Who can explore his strange design?
> In vain the first-born seraph tries
> To sound the depths of love divine
> 'Tis mercy all! let earth adore,
> Let angel minds inquire no more.[5]

What self-sacrificing humility our Lord displayed! We are saved by virtue of his willingness to humble himself and put our interests above his own comfort. We cannot receive the benefits of his sacrifice and then refuse to follow his example.

Paul concludes this section by referring to the third stage of

Christ's experience, namely, his exaltation after coming to this world (vv. 10–11).

Having completed the work of redemption on the cross and having risen from the dead, the Lord Jesus ascended to the Father in heaven (Acts 1:1–11), where he now reigns in exaltation. The Father has given him 'the name which is above every name' (v. 9). Debate swirls around this name, but this is beyond debate: every knee is going to bow in submission before the exalted Christ and every tongue is going to confess that he is Lord of all.

For further study ▶

FOR FURTHER STUDY

1. Paul was fond of using military imagery for the Christian life. Read his words in Ephesians 6:10–20. How does he describe the Christian's enemies? What are the pieces of armour that he identifies?
2. With the phrase 'even the death of the cross' (2:8), Paul indicates the special nature of Jesus' crucifixion. What made the death of Jesus special? Read Galatians 3:13; Romans 5:6–8; Hebrews 9:28; 1 Peter 2:24. Read Psalm 22 and Isaiah 53 for amazingly detailed prophecies of the cross of Christ. What do these prophecies teach about the nature of Christ's death?
3. Read Paul's words in 1 Corinthians 15:24–28 for more about the final and universal subjection to Christ. What is the last enemy to be destroyed? Read Revelation 5. What will the redeemed of all ages sing as they gather around the throne of God?

TO THINK ABOUT AND DISCUSS

1. The gospel is very precisely stated in the Scriptures. In the light of this section, how would you deal with a person who says that the gospel is so ambiguous that it is impossible to discuss it?
2. What practical steps could you, or your church leaders, take to cultivate the spirit of greater unity in your church or fellowship group?

4 Applying the mind of Christ

(2:12–18)

Having described the mind of Christ (vv 5–11), the apostle appeals to his readers to implement it. The word 'therefore' signals conclusion and application

The mind of Christ was one of humble submission to the work of redemption that the Father had set before him. Paul has some work in mind for the Philippians. Would they manifest the mind of Christ by gladly obeying the apostle even though he was absent from them? (v 12).

> Paul wants the Philippians to understand that it is with a heart of love for them

While he is sounding the note of apostolic authority here, Paul wants the Philippians to understand that it is with a heart of love for them. He refers to them as 'my beloved' (v 12). He is calling them to obey him, not because he is an egotist who enjoys issuing orders and flaunting authority, but rather because their obedience will be of benefit to them.

Work out (vv. 12–13)

Paul states the first duty he had in mind with these words: '…work out your own salvation with fear and trembling…' (v. 12).

The apostle is not asking the Philippians to work for their salvation. If we are in doubt about this, we only have to read a bit further. He will soon give details of his own futile efforts to earn the favour of God (3:1–11).

Those who advocate salvation by works do so only because they fail to understand that God demands perfect righteousness of us. When this point hits home, it is obvious to us that we cannot be saved by works, because, no matter how many good works we do, they cannot elevate us to the level of perfect righteousness.

Paul tells his readers to 'work out' their salvation. His meaning becomes clearer when we look at his next phrase: '… for it is God who works in you …' (v. 13).

We noted earlier that salvation is God's work. We cannot save ourselves. Only God can enlighten our minds to see the truth and move our wills to accept the truth. The very faith with which we receive his work of salvation is not something we can produce. It is rather God's gift to us. He gives us both the salvation to receive by faith and the faith to receive the salvation (Eph. 2:8–9). No one who finally enters eternal glory will have one shred of credit to claim. God will not share his glory with another.

Paul was calling the Philippians, therefore, to work out what God had worked in. They were to live in such a way as to manifest that God had done his saving work within them.

They were to show outwardly what God had done inwardly.

While we must not believe in salvation by works, we must most certainly believe in a salvation that works. In other words, we must not fall for that lie of the devil which suggests that one can truly be saved and not manifest it by good works.

This was, of course, the issue with which James was so urgently concerned when he wrote: '... faith by itself, if it does not have works, is dead. But someone will say, "You have faith, and I have works." Show me your faith without your works, and I will show you my faith by my works. You believe that there is one God. You do well. Even the demons believe—and tremble! But do you want to know, O foolish man, that faith without works is dead?' (James 2:17–20).

'You believe that there is one God. You do well. Even the demons believe—and tremble!'

Paul made the same point—that true salvation manifests itself in good works—in these words to the Ephesians: 'For we are His workmanship created in Christ Jesus for good works, which God prepared beforehand that we should walk in them' (Eph. 2:10).

We cannot leave this point without noting that the 'working out' for which the apostle calls is to be done with 'fear and trembling' (v. 12) and also with confidence (v. 13).

With the phrase 'fear and trembling', the apostle was calling his readers to go about their Christian lives with a sense of awe and wonder. The apostle was calling them to manifest in their daily living the salvation of the living God, the salvation that had been planned for them before the foundation of the world. They were part of something that was far more massive than they could imagine. Mundane Christian duties dance and shimmer with delight when we learn to coat them with privilege. And living for the Lord becomes easier when we understand that it is the Lord for whom we live.

Lest his readers should feel overwhelmed by the thought of having to work out their salvation with fear and trembling, Paul added a word of assurance that would give them confidence: '... it is God who works in you both to will and to do his good pleasure' (v. 13).

The God who had done the work of salvation within them had not abandoned them. He was still at work in them, giving them both the desire and the power to work out their salvation. If we have no desire to live for the Lord, we have no right to say we know the Lord.

Shine forth (vv. 14–18)

Here Paul adds a second duty. The Philippians were to 'do all things without complaining and disputing' (v 14). They were to do this so that they could 'become blameless and harmless, children of God without fault in the midst of a crooked and perverse generation' (v. 15).

Paul is not saying that they would become children of God by avoiding complaining and disputing. They were already children of God. His point is rather that they would become known as children of God by avoiding these things.

Certain things are simply out of keeping with the Christian faith, and when unbelievers see these things in us, they are quick to conclude that there is nothing to our

Christianity. Complaining and grumbling are certainly among those things.

Christians believe that God is sovereign over all things, including even those circumstances that they find unpleasant and undesirable. When we complain and grumble, we are telling those around us that we believe God is doing a very poor job, and, if given the opportunity, we could do much better.

If we are not on our guard, grumbling can become a way of life with us: the weather is not what we would like it to be; people don't treat us the way they should; the church leaders don't handle things correctly; and so the list could go on!

We can regard such grumbling as harmless and inevitable, but the God who found it so revolting in Israel of old is every bit as displeased with it today as he was then (1 Cor. 10:10–11).

We can go a long way towards conquering grumbling and complaining by keeping constantly in mind the world in which we live...

We can go a long way towards conquering grumbling and complaining by keeping constantly in mind the world in which we live, and our responsibility in it. This world is a dark place—it is both 'crooked' and 'perverse' (v. 15). This world is not as God made it. It has been warped and twisted by sin, but God's people are not like the world. We are those in whom the darkness has been dispelled by the light of the gospel, and we are now to 'shine as lights in the world' (v. 15).

How do we, as God's people, shine in this world? Paul says

it is by 'holding fast the word of life' (v. 16).

Some suggest it is better to translate 'holding fast' as 'holding forth.' God's people dispel the darkness of sin by spreading the gospel of Christ. But we can't 'talk up' the gospel with tongues that are usually employed in 'talking down'.

Paul was an extraordinary man for several reasons, one of which was that he always kept eternity in view. He urged the Philippians to heed his words and discharge their duties so that on the day of Christ's return he would be able to look with satisfaction upon the work he, Paul, had bestowed on them (v. 16).

Even the thought of laying down his life brought the apostle tremendous joy, especially if the pouring out of his blood could be considered as 'a drink offering.'

In the Old Testament era, drink offerings were poured out by the priests on top of animal sacrifices (Num. 15:1–10). Alec Motyer writes: 'The regulations for this part of the sacrificial system are not absolutely clear, but we can at least say that the drink offering was the accompaniment of a larger sacrifice; it was the small thing which brought a major offering to completeness.'[1]

Paul seems to be saying, therefore, that if he had to die, he would be happy to regard it as 'the finishing touch'[2] to their lives of service and sacrifice.

FOR FURTHER STUDY

1. Read Romans 4. Was Abraham saved by grace through faith, or by works? If Abraham was saved by works, would God receive the glory or would it go to Abraham? (see v. 2). Is it true that grace and works are mutually exclusive, that if we are saved by grace, it cannot be by works, and vice versa?
2. Paul's words 'shine as lights' should remind us of Matthew 5:14–16. What is the result of Christians shining as God's lights? (see 1 Peter 2:9–12). Where do believers get their light? Read John 8:12.

TO THINK ABOUT AND DISCUSS

1. It has been said that 'all we contribute to our salvation is our sin'. Discuss this statement in the light of the foregoing section of Scripture.
2. If you are a Christian, God is at work in you, enabling you to work out your salvation. Discuss this point in the light of the works he has planned for you to do, and the obstacles you may have to overcome, including trials and temptations.
3. You know a Christian who often grumbles. How would you use this passage to help him or her to make some changes in behaviour?

5 The mind of Christ exemplified

(2:19–29)

It will be helpful to us to remember that Paul was writing a letter to the Philippians. We have all written letters and we know what it is to jump very quickly from some thoughts that have been going through our heads to describe something that has happened to us or something we are planning to do. We do not write letters to those we love with great concern for literary technique; we write to express our love from the overflow of our hearts

With these verses Paul suddenly shifts his attention from the sublime doctrine he has been expounding to his plans for the Philippians. Some are troubled by this shift. They try to enforce some sort of order here, showing that Paul really intended these practical concerns to be an extension and illustration of the doctrine he has been expounding. Others suggest that the inclusion of these practical concerns at this particular point indicate that the letter has been tampered with, and if we possessed the original document we would find this section at the end with other such matters.

But such suggestions flow from a desire for tidiness that letter-writers do not share.

On the other hand, we also have to remember that there is another dynamic at work here. While Paul was writing a letter, the Spirit of God was carrying him along to the point that his letter was also the Word of God. While Paul himself, then, may not have intended these verses to continue his theme, we can see that the Spirit of God so ordered them in that way that Timothy and Epaphroditus became models of the mind of Christ.

Timothy (vv. 19–24)

The apostle announces his plans to send Timothy to Philippi soon. He writes: 'I trust in the Lord Jesus Christ to send Timothy to you shortly…' (v. 19).

By so stating his intention, the apostle was registering his conviction that human plans are always subject to the sovereign will of the Lord. Man proposes but God disposes.

Timothy's visit would have the double benefit of relaying information to the church about Paul's situation and, of course, on his return to Paul, relaying information about the church (v. 19).

Paul's next statements are the ones that leap off the page and catch the eye: 'For I have no one like-minded, who will sincerely care for your state. For all seek their own, not the things which are of Christ Jesus' (vv. 20–21).

These sad words make us wonder about the situation in

which Paul found himself. Were Christians in Rome so lacking in spirituality that he could find absolutely no one but Timothy to undertake a mission that required the ability to discern and encourage?

Or was Paul's focus more narrow? Was he only saying that out of the handful of men who were available to him for this assignment only Timothy had the credentials?

...our churches are filled with commotion and emotion...

We do not know. But this we do know: his words are like a splash of ice cold water in the face. We can't read them without wondering what he would say about us. Would he look at our churches and say: 'all seek their own, not the things which are of Christ Jesus'?

Many of us know there is very little of Christ in much of so-called Christendom. Someone has observed that our churches are filled with commotion and emotion but there is little devotion, that is, devotion to Christ.[1]

It is very easy to pay lip-service to Christ-centredness and not be Christ-centred. It is very easy to think we are being Christ-centred while we are really being self-centred. To see this one needs only to listen to the words of many popular Christian songs. Because they use the name of Jesus, we may think they are Christ-centred, but upon closer inspection they prove to be about us and what we are feeling and experiencing. It sometimes seems that 'Christendom' would be better called 'Us-endom.'

It is sadly possible for pastors to use the name of Jesus regularly without really preaching Jesus. We can talk about the Jesus whose primary concern is to be a friend to us and help us cope with the aggravations of life. But is this truly preaching Christ? What about his sovereign deity? What about his incarnation and his sinless life? What about his functioning as prophet, priest and king? What about his atoning death and his resurrection and on-going intercession? Can Christ truly be preached when these central truths are virtually ignored?

Paul's sad words about living for self rather than Christ should drive all of us to examine ourselves. Warren Wiersbe observes: 'In a very real sense, all of us live either in Philippians 1:21 or Philippians 2:21.'[2]

Epaphroditus (vv. 25–29)

The man (v. 25)

We know very little about Epaphroditus. His name appears only in Philippians. But although his time in the galaxy of Scripture is very brief, he leaves a lasting impression. He is like a meteor that shines briefly but brilliantly.

The name Epaphroditus means 'charming,' and he was indeed a charming man. Paul was obviously charmed by him, and we should be as well.

The love Paul had for him is reflected in the terms he used to describe him.

- **'MY BROTHER'**—This term is a testimony to the affection Paul felt for this man. It is also a testimony to the marvel of God's grace. Paul and Epaphroditus were very different by nature, the former being a Jew and the latter a Greek. But the grace of God had made them part of the same family, the family of God. Natural distinctions and barriers had been broken down to the point that these men enjoyed a oneness in Christ.

- **'FELLOW-WORKER'**—In addition to sharing the warmth of brotherhood, Paul and Epaphroditus shared the responsibility of Christian labour. Their labour reminds us that God has called all his people to industrious effort on behalf of his kingdom. It is a privilege to be a labourer for God. Christians will be brothers and sisters forever, but they can only be fellow-workers in the church for a few short years.
- **'FELLOW-SOLDIER'**—Epaphroditus understood that he and Paul were not only involved in work but also in war. He would have sounded a hearty 'Amen!' to the military terminology Paul had already used (1:27–28). He would also agree with what Paul would go on to write about enemies of the faith (3:18). But, unlike so many Christians, Epaphroditus was not one to shrink from standing for Christ and his truth. He believed so strongly in the value of the gospel that he was willing to contend for it (Jude 3).

What happened to the man (vv. 25–28)

Epaphroditus' willingness to serve the Lord is readily apparent in these verses. He had been sent by the Philippian church to bear to Rome a gift for Paul and to minister to him (v. 25). While he was there, he fell ill. We should not pass over this detail quickly. Some would have us believe that Christians should never be sick (or at least not for very long) and if a Christian does become sick, they say, he should simply claim healing by faith and it will be his. If he fails to have such healing, they reason, it is because he is deficient in faith.

But here are Epaphroditus and Paul, who obviously are men of great faith, and Epaphroditus becomes ill. And there is no healing. To the contrary, the illness is such that Epaphroditus almost dies (v. 27).

Here, however, is the measure of the man: while he is so seriously ill, his thoughts are not for himself but rather for his dear brothers and sisters in Christ in Philippi.

While Epaphroditus was not instantaneously healed from his illness, he was sustained by God through it and eventually recovered, much to the delight of the apostle (v. 27). Paul then sent him back to the church with, we presume, this letter in his hand.

How the man should be regarded (vv. 29–30)

Paul wanted the Philippians to receive Epaphroditus with great joy and appreciation for his faithful ministry on their behalf and with gratitude to God for preserving his life. Above all that, Paul wants them to esteem him because of his spirit—the spirit of laying aside his own comfort and convenience for the cause of Christ (v. 30). Epaphroditus serves, therefore, as another example of one who was seized by the mind of Christ.

The major lesson for us to learn here is that the people of God are not to take faithful servants of Christ for granted but rather to hold them in high esteem. Paul strikes this note in his first letter to the Thessalonians: 'And we urge you, brethren, to recognize those who labour among you, and are over you in the Lord and admonish you, and to esteem them very highly in love for their work's sake. Be at peace among yourselves' (1 Thess. 5:12–13).

FOR FURTHER STUDY

1. What do the following Scriptures teach us about Timothy's background: Acts 16:1–3; 2 Timothy 1:5; 3:15?
2. Read 1 Corinthians 2:1–5. Was Paul determined to have a Christ-centred ministry? Why? Read Colossians 1:13–18. Why is Christ entitled to pre-eminence?
3. What do the following Scriptures identify as actions that manifest proper regard for a godly, Christ-preaching pastor: 1 Timothy 5:17–19; Hebrews 13:7,17–18.

TO THINK ABOUT AND DISCUSS

1. This section challenges us to Christ-centred living. It is so easy to seek the things which are our own, and not 'the things which are of Christ Jesus'. By putting the Lord Jesus Christ first in all of life, in what ways do you think people's lives may be changed? Consider this question with specific reference to

- Financial giving
- Hospitality
- Practical acts of compassion such as hospital visitation, care for widows, ministry to prisoners, etc.

2. Ephaphroditus was sick and almost died. How does this account illustrate God's complete control over sickness, healing and death?
3. For private or personal application: Think of a few ways in which you could cultivate some of the fine qualities of Timothy and Ephaphroditus into your own life, to the benefit and blessing of other people.

6 A warning about confidence in the flesh

(3:1–11)

When he was summing up one point and ready to move to another, the great preacher, Dr Martyn Lloyd-Jones, would often say: 'Very well, then...'[1] This meant he was wrapping up his consideration of one matter and moving to another

The word translated 'Finally' (v. 1) means much the same. It does not mean that the apostle was intending to conclude his letter. Rather, he was moving to another subject. Some translate the word 'For the rest…'. In other words, they understand Paul to be saying something like this: 'Now that we have considered this matter, let us turn our attention to what remains.'

What remained in this instance was for Paul to call the Philippians to rejoice in the Lord (v. 1). While the apostle himself has expressed joy throughout this letter, this is his first exhortation to the Philippians to rejoice.

It seems that Paul issues this exhortation only then immediately to lose sight of it and move to something totally unrelated, that is, warning against false teachers. I suggest, however, that there is more order here than we might think at first sight. Immediately after calling his readers to rejoice in the Lord, the apostle begins warning them about confidence in the flesh. One cannot rejoice in the Lord and at the same time rejoice in the flesh. The two are mutually exclusive.

> One cannot rejoice in the Lord and at the same time rejoice in the flesh. The two are mutually exclusive

This warning would not have been necessary if it had not been for the presence of certain false teachers who were flesh-promoters *par excellence*. These teachers we know as Judaizers. They believed that faith in Jesus as the Messiah was not enough for salvation, that one also had to keep the law of Moses, and, in particular, submit to the Mosaic requirement of circumcision. Theirs was, then, a 'Jesus-plus' religion. To be saved, one had to have Jesus plus works. While, as we have previously noticed, it is an error to say one can be saved and not manifest it in good works, it is also an error to say that one can be saved through good works.

The warning stated (vv. 2–3)

The apostle refuses to mince words in sounding his alarm. He writes: 'Beware of dogs, beware of evil workers, beware of the mutilation!' (v. 2).

He has previously warned about false teachers (1:28–29).

Now he warns about a particular kind of false teacher. He regards false teaching to be such a danger that it is impossible to mention it too frequently (v. 1b).

His words are cause for pause. To hear many tell it, there is little if any danger from false teachers. Many, because they cannot believe that there is any such thing as truth, cannot believe in false teachers. They have no 'beware' in their religion. There is no danger, so there is no need for caution and vigilance.

Dogs

Such people find themselves astonished that Paul could write in such blunt, unvarnished terms. How could he call these teachers 'dogs'? He did so because of certain obvious similarities between the two:

- as the dogs roamed the streets seeking something to eat, so the false teachers roamed about while looking for opportunities to spread their teachings;
- as the dogs were sly and cunning, so were the teachers;
- as the dogs represented a danger to those who encountered them, so the teachers represented spiritual danger to their hearers.

Evil workers

With this term, the apostle may have intended to convey how very diligent the Judaizers were in spreading their doctrines. They were not lazy and indolent slackers, but busy workers. But while they advocated good works as the means for attaining salvation, they were, in fact, doing evil works. Any teaching that denies the redeeming work of the Lord Jesus or any way detracts from it has the apostolic description stamped upon it for ever—evil!

This part of Paul's description ought to cause us pain. So often the purveyors of false doctrines are so much more devoted to their task than are believers of the true gospel.

The mutilation

The Judaizers believed that the circumcision of the flesh required by the law of Moses was essential for salvation. Paul decisively repudiates and rejects this teaching by calling such teachers 'the mutilation.' The circumcision of the Mosaic law was intended to be the outer manifestation of the true circumcision, which was of the heart. In other words, true circumcision consisted of the painful breaking away from sin with a truly repentant heart (Lev. 26:41; Deut. 10:16; 30:6; Jer. 4:4). If this inner reality was missing, the outer manifestation of it amounted to nothing more than mutilation of the body.

When it comes to this matter of standing clean before a holy God, circumcision amounts to nothing more than mere mutilation of the flesh. It has absolutely no spiritual value.

After describing the false teachers in such a graphic way, the apostle quickly adds that he and his fellow-believers in Christ are the true circumcision (v. 3). He characterizes believers as those who:

- **WORSHIP GOD IN THE SPIRIT**—no operation on the flesh can produce true worship of God which is spiritual in nature;
- **REJOICE IN CHRIST JESUS**—William Hendriksen writes: 'Those whose hearts—hence also lips and ears—have been circumcised make their boast in the Lord, in him

alone. Such boasters rely entirely on Christ Jesus, the Anointed Savior; on his *person* and *work*. They glory in his *cross*, that is, in his atonement, as the only basis for their salvation';[2]

- **HAVE NO CONFIDENCE IN THE FLESH**—Hendriksen explains: 'In broad terms, *flesh is anything apart from Christ on which one bases his hope for salvation*'.[3] The believer, understanding that there is absolutely nothing that he can do with his body to earn salvation, trusts in Christ and Christ alone.

The warning reinforced by personal testimony (vv. 4–11)

Paul's former dependence on the flesh (vv. 4–6)

Paul here supports the warning he has issued with the details of his own experience. If anyone had reason to trust in the works of the flesh for salvation, it was he (v. 4). He was circumcised when he was eight days old, just as the law of Moses required. He was born into the nation of Israel and into the tribe of Benjamin. All of this meant that he, Paul, was 'a Hebrew of the Hebrews' or 'a Hebrew beyond question'.

In addition to these things, Paul had become a member of the Pharisees, who were known for their high regard for the law of Moses. He had also displayed unquestioned zeal for Judaism, going so far as to persecute Christians, whom he regarded as a threat to it. His performance was such that all those who had known him and observed him would have to say that he was blameless in every way.

Paul's point is that few of the Judaizers could match his

record, and none of them could surpass it. As far as depending on the flesh was concerned, Paul was the 'depender' *par excellence*.

Paul's repudiation of the flesh (vv. 7–9)

Paul's confidence in his good works came to a sudden stop when he realized that despite all he had done he had still fallen far short of what God demanded.

And what does God demand of sinners? It is all wrapped up in the word 'righteousness' (v. 9). God is a holy and righteous God, and heaven is a holy and righteous place. God has made it clear that nothing that is unrighteous or defiling will ever enter there (Rev. 21:27).

Now Paul had a kind of righteousness, 'a righteousness which is from the law' (v. 9). He is referring to the law of Moses. This law, given to the nation of Israel by God, describes and details for us the righteousness which God demands of all who would enter heaven. It's all perfectly summarized in the Ten Commandments (Exod. 20:1–17). If a person could perfectly keep this law, that person would be indeed righteous in the eyes of God.

God is a holy and righteous God, and heaven is a holy and righteous place

Paul thought he had kept this law, and those who observed him would no doubt have agreed. But the righteousness Paul had was not the kind of 'law righteousness' God demanded. It was not perfect obedience to every single demand of the law. It was 'law righteousness' in an external fashion only.

Paul spells this out in Romans 7:7–11. There he says he

came to understand that his keeping of the law was in an external fashion only and God's demand for perfect righteousness was so radical and thorough that it included even internal desires. This hit Paul with devastating impact. He realized that all he had done was in the way of external works, that internally he had not really kept the law of God and, therefore, fell far short of God's demand for perfect righteousness. When Paul understood these things he counted all his own righteousness as worse than useless, as mere rubbish (v. 8).

Paul's new dependence on Christ (vv. 9–11)

This brought Paul to despair, but then, by the grace of God, he saw something else: God himself had provided in Jesus Christ the very righteousness that he, God, demands. Jesus Christ is the only one who had true 'law righteousness.' He came to this earth in our humanity and lived in perfect obedience to God's laws. He did not break any of them in word, thought or deed. Sinners can stand acceptably only before God if they are clothed in the righteousness of Christ. This righteousness is:

- **FROM GOD (V. 9).** God the Father and Christ the Son were in agreement on the plan of redemption. Christ did not come to do something the Father did not want done. It was God the Father who sent Christ to this world to provide the righteousness sinners need.
- **THROUGH FAITH (V. 9).** Because Christ provides the righteousness we need, there is absolutely nothing we can do to add to it. That would be like striking a match to help

the sun shine. We can only receive the righteousness he has provided.

After receiving from Christ the fulfilment of his greatest longing—the longing for righteousness—Paul found himself with a new longing, namely, the longing to know this Christ in an intimate way. Paul wanted to know in particular the power of Christ's resurrection and the fellowship of his sufferings (v. 10). He wanted to experience in his own life the power that had raised Christ from the dead. He wanted that kind of power to be at work in his life. He even wanted to share Christ's crucifixion. Christ was crucified as a sacrifice for sin. Paul's desire to share in Christ's crucifixion must mean, therefore, that he yearned to see sin die more and more in his life. This desire makes perfect sense because sin hinders us from growing in the knowledge of God.

Paul also yearned for the day when he would be raised from the dead (v. 11). Only then would the redemption Christ has provided for him be complete and his knowledge of Christ would be perfect. The contemplation of that day would undoubtedly have caused Paul to endorse these words most heartily from Fanny J. Crosby:

Then I shall see him face to face
And tell the story 'Saved by grace'.[4]

FOR FURTHER STUDY

1. Read 2 Peter 2:1–22 and Jude. What are some of the main characteristics of false teachers? Read 2 John 7–11. How are God's people to respond to false teachers?
2. Read John 6:63. What does the Lord Jesus Christ have to say about dependence on the flesh? Read Romans 8:5–9. What does the apostle Paul say about the flesh pleasing God?
3. Read John 1:18; 1 Peter 1:19; 1 John 3:5. Did Jesus lead a sinless life? Why is this important?

TO THINK ABOUT AND DISCUSS

1. There is only one way to be saved: God's way. Man's way can never succeed. Suggest a few modern religious systems which contradict the clear teaching of the apostle in this passage.
2. What evangelistic approaches would you use in helping such people to understand the true gospel of God's grace?

7 Passionately pursuing

(3:12–16)

These verses continue the testimony Paul began in verse 4. He first spoke about the past in which he had abandoned all confidence in his own works and trusted in Christ alone for salvation

Now he shares with the Philippians his present experience. It was one of passionately pursuing a distinct goal. We can divide this portion of his testimony into the following parts: Paul's goal, Paul's pursuit, and Paul's exhortations.

Paul's goal

What was the goal of Paul's life? He says it was to 'lay hold of that for which Christ Jesus has also laid hold of me' (v. 12).

Paul was keenly aware of Christ laying hold of him. He, Paul, was riding along to Damascus, secure in his belief that he was doing God a service by persecuting Christians. Suddenly, he was blinded by a bright light and knocked to the ground. There in the dust he heard the voice of the risen Christ. He realized that the Jesus he so despised was indeed the Christ, and that in persecuting Christians, he was in fact persecuting Christ (Acts 9:1–9).

'Laying hold' is an appropriate term for what happened to Paul (then known as Saul of Tarsus). He was there seized with the strong, unbreakable grip of the risen, sovereign Lord.

Paul also knew that the Lord Jesus had a purpose in so seizing him. Yes, it was to make him a special messenger to the Gentiles (Acts 9:15). But it was for the purpose which Paul has already stated: 'that I may know him' (v. 10).

> Paul also knew that the Lord Jesus had a purpose in so seizing him...'that I may know him'

The Lord Jesus seized and saved Paul in order to bring him into an intimate knowledge of himself, a knowledge that would increase throughout Paul's life and culminate in perfect knowledge at death.

This goal was also, therefore, to realize 'the prize of the upward call of God in Christ Jesus' (v. 14).

Paul's goal was, then, to keep moving up and up in his knowledge of and fellowship with the Lord until he could finally hear the Lord say: 'Come up here' (Rev. 4:1; 11:12).

We must not leave this point without taking time to note that, while believers do not all experience the sensational elements present in Paul's conversion, they are all without exception laid hold of by God, who opens their minds to see their sin and the sufficiency of Christ, and who grants them faith.

Are we as Christians conscious to the degree that we

should be, that we have an 'upward call?' This is a call from heaven that will finally take us to heaven. It is a call that beckons us to keep moving forward and upward in our knowledge of the Lord.

Paul's pursuit

The wonder and glory of this call so captured Paul's heart that he could not be passive or casual about it. Had Christ laid hold of him for such a high purpose? Then he, Paul, would respond by seeking to lay hold of that purpose. Had Christ laid hold of him to bring him into intimate knowledge of himself? Then Paul would respond by fervently, passionately seeking that knowledge.

What is necessary to reach this goal? Paul answers by using the illustration of a runner. What must the runner do to succeed? He must not concern himself with some awkward mistake or misstep at the beginning of the race. He cannot run well if he is thinking about how poorly he broke from the blocks, or, on the other hand, how splendidly he covered the first few yards. He must be good at obliteration, wiping such thoughts from his mind. And he must focus his concentration completely on the goal line, driving towards it with everything his body has to offer and straining every muscle.

Here is a picture for every Christian to etch into his or her mind. We must approach the Christian life in the same manner. We must not look back to our failures or successes. We must keep ever in mind that our goal is to know Christ better, and we must daily put forth the effort to reach that goal.

We admire this kind of devotion in every area of life except the spiritual realm. When Olympic athletes begin to discipline their bodies and hone their skills, we heap praise upon them. When someone shows total dedication in the areas of medicine, science, music or drama, we approve and applaud. We applaud, for example, the violinist who explained her success in this way: 'I deliberately planned to neglect everything else until my practice period was completed. That program of planned neglect accounts for my success.'

But when we hear of someone doing this in the area of Christian living, we are inclined to dismiss him as something of a fanatic, who, as someone has observed, will not change his mind and will not change the subject.

> We often embrace the 'shotgun' approach to life...scattering our time and energies...

Why do those who are focused on knowing God bother us? Is it not because they remind us that our own priorities are not what they ought to be? Most people are living such cluttered, distracted and fragmented lives. Our lives are not integrated around a single, unifying purpose. We often embrace the 'shotgun' approach to life, trying to find happiness and satisfaction by scattering our time and energies over a wide range of interests and activities. We want to try a little bit of everything, and we do not want to miss out on anything.

Paul suggests we use the 'rifle' approach by finding the singular priority that makes life worth living, that is, the Lord Jesus Christ, and give ourselves unreservedly to it. He would have us say in the words of the hymn:

I'm pressing on the upward way,
New heights I'm gaining every day;
Still praying as I onward bound,
Lord, plant my feet on higher ground.[1]

Paul knew he had not, and would not, perfectly achieve his goal of intimately knowing Christ in this life. He writes: 'Brethren, I do not count myself to have apprehended...' (v. 13). But he would at least come before his Lord as one who strenuously pressed toward the goal. May God help each of us to come before the Lord in the same way!

Paul's appeals (vv. 15–16)

In a race, only one can win, but in the Christian race, all can. Paul, therefore, urges all his readers to join him in vigorously running. He appeals to them to 'have this mind' (v. 15).

Some in the church of Philippi may have thought they had already attained perfection, but the mature believers there knew better (v. 15). Paul intended to leave to the Lord those who were mistaken about their progress in spiritual things. The apostle knew the Lord had straightened him out on many issues and could be counted on to do the same with the perfectionists in Philippi.

Paul closes this section with this exhortation: '... to the degree that we have already attained, let us walk by the same rule, let us be of the same mind' (v. 16).

In other words, they were to examine their lives and identify periods of progress they had made in spiritual things. When they found times of spiritual attainment, they were to recall the spirit they had when that attainment came about and apply that same spirit now. Marvin R. Vincent puts it in these words: 'Whatever real Christian and moral attainment you may have made, let that serve as a rule for your further advance'.[2]

The passage we have examined is more than remarkable. Think about Paul for a moment: he had walked with God for several years; he had enjoyed great spiritual experiences; he knew God so well that he could write glorious spiritual truths that have overwhelmed and awed the best theological minds of the centuries; he could stare death in the face without flinching. And yet he says he was still straining to know the Lord Jesus better. If the apostle, with all that he had attained, felt this need, how much more should we?

For further study ▶

FOR FURTHER STUDY

1. Read Jeremiah 9:23–24. Is the knowledge of God more important than riches and power? Where does it rank on your scale of priorities?
2. Read Colossians 1:9–10. Is it possible for Christians to increase in the knowledge of God? Suggest what this might mean to you in practice.
3. Paul developed the race imagery in 1 Corinthians 9:24–27 and 2 Timothy 2:5. What is the prize for which the Christian runs? What does Paul say about how he was running? What does he say to Timothy about running? Read Hebrews 12:1–2. What does this author tell us about the Christian race?

TO THINK ABOUT AND DISCUSS

1. Godly Christians who have lived before us recognized that the three main enemies believers face are the world, the flesh and the devil. Suggest some specific examples in each of these arenas which may hinder you from passionately pursuing the goal of becoming more and more like Christ.
2. Paul's analogy of the runner suggests the need for a Christian to engage in diligent self-control and to have a careful focus on living a godly life. In what specific areas of life do you think you could apply some of these principles? You may wish to use the following categories:

- Lifestyle
- Relationships
- Bible reading, prayer (private and public), worship and fellowship
- Financial resources and stewardship in the Lord's work

8 Following the right example

(3:17–4:1)

Getting to know God well is a difficult and demanding business. What should we do when we find ourselves facing a challenge that seems too difficult for us? We should do what the unsure guest does when he is at one of those fancy dinners and doesn't know which fork to use: we should find a good role model and do what that person does

Wherever we turn in the Bible, we find the importance of good role models stressed. The example of Lot immediately comes to mind. When it became necessary for him to part company with Abraham, he made the decision to move in with the ungodly citizens of Sodom. It wasn't long until disaster struck! (Gen. 13:1–13; 19:1–29).

Perhaps Paul had Lot in mind when he wrote to the Corinthians: 'Do not be deceived: Evil company corrupts good habits' (1 Cor. 15:33).

If we want to know the Lord Jesus Christ better, one of the best things we can do is to find and follow people who know him very well. To do this means we keep our distance from those who are the enemies of God. We can't follow people going in opposite directions.

In these verses, the apostle Paul draws a vivid contrast between his example and the example of those who are anti-God in their attitudes and actions.

The godly example of Paul (v. 17)

It troubles some that Paul uses himself as an example for the Philippians to follow. It seems like a proud and boastful thing. However, we won't stumble at this point if we keep a few things in mind: First, Paul tells the Philippians to follow him only after candidly confessing he was far from perfect (v. 12). In now holding himself up as an example, Paul isn't suddenly going back on what he has just said. Even though he was dissatisfied with the progress he had made in getting to know God, at least he knew what was involved in knowing God better and he was earnestly striving to that end. This was enough to make him a positive example for them.

'Be imitators of me...'

Secondly, Paul has already told the Philippians that their chief example in all things is the Lord Jesus Christ himself (2:5). The fact he now tells them to follow him means he is here repeating what he said to the Corinthians: 'Be imitators of me, as I also am of Christ' (1 Cor. 11:1).

By putting it in these terms, Paul makes it clear he is not asking anyone to follow him blindly, no matter what he does, but to follow him only so far as his life corresponds to the teachings of Christ.

Thirdly, we need to remember that Paul was an apostle of the Lord Jesus Christ. This means he had received a special calling and was a special emissary for the Lord. Serving as an example to others was part and parcel of the apostle's calling.

It was all very well and good for the Philippians to follow Paul's example, but where does this leave us? The apostles have long since departed this earthly arena. However, even though we don't have the apostles themselves, we still have access to their lives and teachings through the Bible. For us to follow the apostles' teachings and way of life means being earnestly enthusiastic about the Bible. We should be daily reading it, meditating upon it, praying over it, and seeking to practise it.

Thank God, we, too, are not completely without the example of godly men and women since the time of the apostles. Such examples may be found in biographies, and even in the lives of many around us. The examples of godliness are there. It's our responsibility to look for them and to pattern our lives after them.

After calling the Philippians to follow his example, Paul warns them about the example of the ungodly.

The example of the ungodly (vv. 18–19)

Paul warns the Philippians about certain people who were evidently great in number ('many') and of whom he had warned them frequently before. These weren't people who had merely slipped into error, but rather believed it and practised it (the word 'walk' denotes an ongoing way of life).

Of whom was Paul writing at this particular point? Some think he had the Judaizers in mind. Others think he was referring to Gentiles who had professed faith in Christ but were living in a grossly sensual and immoral manner.

Perhaps it is good that Paul left the identity of these people vague. Had he clearly identified a certain group, we might connect the danger only with that one group and forget that false teaching and sinful living can come at us from any side.

Most Christians don't seem to take the danger of heresy very seriously

Most Christians don't seem to take the danger of heresy very seriously. We have a 'live and let live' mentality. Mention heresy, and someone will quickly say we have no right to tell others what they should believe and how they should behave. But when people profess to be Christians we have every right to expect them to subscribe to the clear teachings of the Bible and order their lives accordingly.

Paul would not take kindly to our softness on doctrinal and moral purity. It was such a serious matter to him that he actually wept as he wrote of it (v. 18). We may like preachers to be entertaining comedians, but Paul took spiritual matters with a deadly earnestness.

Was Paul just an emotionally feeble character who finally caved in under the stress and strain of ministry? Was he suffering from ministerial burnout to the degree that he could no longer control his emotions? Hardly. Paul saw doctrinal heretics and people holding to moral error for what they really are—enemies of the cross of Jesus Christ.

How precious was the cross to Paul! He knew he owed his salvation to nothing less than the Lord Jesus Christ going there and receiving the penalty for his sin. The cross was so central to Paul that he had absolutely no patience with any doctrine that in any way minimized it or disparaged it. How were these errant people disparaging the cross? We will see in the next section, but suffice it to say that anyone who teaches that one can be saved and go on living in the very sin from which Christ died to deliver us is attacking the innermost meaning of the cross!

How do we regard the cross of Christ? Is it precious to us? Are we jealous over it to the point that we will not tolerate any belief or behaviour that belittles it?

Those who don't take the cross of Jesus seriously would do well to take a close look at what Paul says next about enemies of the cross, namely, that their end is destruction (v. 19).

Eternal and irreversible separation from God—that's what Paul means by destruction!

What does this mean? Paul himself defines it in his second letter to the Thessalonians: 'These shall be punished with everlasting destruction from the presence of the Lord and from the glory of His power' (2 Thess. 1:9).

Eternal and irreversible separation from God and all that is good—that's what Paul means by destruction!

'But I don't believe in a God like that,' is the cry of multitudes today. However that has absolutely nothing to do with it! We are not free to decide what kind of God we can live with or accept. God has revealed himself to be a holy God who will bring dreadful judgement upon all those who do not know Jesus Christ as Lord and Saviour. Like it or not, this is the way he is!

From this general warning about these enemies of the cross, Paul goes on to give three ways his readers could identify them.

Their god

First, he says their god is their 'belly' (v. 19). That means they worship their fleshly desires and appetites. Their sole purpose in living is to gratify the lusts of their flesh. Instead of controlling their appetites they allow their appetites to control them.

Their glory

Secondly, Paul says they glory in their shame (v. 19). Their moral values are so topsy-turvy and confused, they actually go around boasting of things they ought to be ashamed of!

One of the surest signs of an individual or a society being utterly decadent is that of not being able to feel shame. When people take it a step further and begin to boast of shameful things, they are perilously close to being completely beyond hope.

What does this tell us about our own society? Boasting about prowess in drinking and in making sexual conquests! Proclaiming sexual perversion as a normal and even desirable way of life! Slaughtering the unborn in the name of freedom and choice! All of these are shameful beyond description, but our society is not ashamed! Instead it tries to make those who condemn such things feel ashamed. It calls perversion normal and common morality abnormal, and all the while God's judgement rumbles in the background. Let someone mention that judgement and he is roundly condemned as something of a religious fanatic and as a very cruel and unfeeling person. What a strange society! It shames those who talk of judgement and refuses to be ashamed of the sin that brings the judgement.

Their mind

The final mark Paul gives of godless people is they set their minds on earthly things (v. 19). They live as though God is dead, as though heaven and hell are myths, and as though this life is all there is.

Paul cannot sustain this litany of gloom any longer. He moves to a glorious contrast. He and the Philippians were, by the grace of God, in a different position. Paul glories in the following:

- **CITIZENSHIP IN HEAVEN (V. 20).** While the Christian is a citizen of this world, his true citizenship, his true home, is in heaven. Unlike the enemies of the cross Paul has been describing, the Christian knows that this world is not the end. It is a travelling place to another world and not a stopping place.
- **THE COMING SAVIOUR (VV. 20–21).** The Lord Jesus Christ will return from heaven one day to engage in triumphant work. He will raise the bodies of believers from the grave and will change those bodies so they will be 'conformed to his glorious body' (v. 21). He will also catch up the saints who are living at the time of his return and will instantaneously

change their bodies so they will also be like him (1 Thess. 4:13–18). All of this will be accomplished by Christ's power, which is so great that it will finally subdue all things (v. 21, see also 1 Cor. 15:28).

God's people are faced with treacherous enemies, but the glories that await them are of such a nature that, as Paul points out with great affection, they should 'stand fast in the Lord' (4:1).

We have in this passage, then, two examples laid before us, and we must be discerning and careful. It is our responsibility to select the right example, follow it, and to resist the pull of the wrong examples.

There is no way the Christian can avoid the tension and struggle of trying to live a godly life

This is not what many Christians want to hear. They want to think the Christian life is easy, but it isn't. There is no way the Christian can avoid the tension and struggle of trying to live a godly life. Like Israel of old, the Christian constantly finds himself between the way of blessing and the way of cursing (Deut. 27:1–28:68). We can follow the example of Paul and find the blessing, or we can follow the example of the enemies of the cross and find cursing. Which will you select as your role model?

FOR FURTHER STUDY

1. Read 1 Corinthians 1:18; 2:1–2 and Galatians 6:14. How did Paul regard the cross of Christ?
2. How is the Christian to respond to the lusts of the flesh? Read 2 Timothy 2:22; Titus 2:12; 1 Peter 2:22; 4:2.
3. In Romans 1:32, the apostle Paul refers to approving of those who do shameful things. Read the preceding verses in this passage (beginning with v. 18). What shameful things did he have in mind?

TO THINK ABOUT AND DISCUSS

1. Some groups and people have taught that, even as a Christian, you can still indulge in sin and live a life which is hardly any different from that of an unbeliever. Discuss this in the light of the teaching in this section.
2. A mentor is someone who sets an example to others and teaches them. Is there someone whom you could mentor, by modelling and demonstrating the grace of God in your life? How would you plan to go about this process?

9 Important instructions

(4:2–9)

Paul's appeal to the Philippians to 'stand fast in the Lord' (4:1) made it possible for him to make a seamless transition to further exhortations, all of which would constitute the matter of standing fast. These exhortations or instructions fall quite naturally into two parts: individual and general

Individual instructions (vv. 2–3)

To two women (v. 2)

In these verses, the apostle addresses two women in the church. He writes: 'I implore Euodia and I implore Syntyche to be of the same mind in the Lord' (v. 2).

Michael Bentley offers these thought-provoking words about this appeal:

> If in one hundred years' time, your name was to be discovered mentioned in an old document, what one thing would you like the finder to learn about you? Would you like it to be recorded that you were a very kind and loving person, or that you were a mature Christian, or that you were good at making people feel at ease?
>
> Two ladies from the church at Philippi have gone down in history, and the thing they are remembered for is that they had fallen out with each other. No one today knows what these women disagreed about. Paul does not say what the problem was, although presumably everyone else in the church at the time knew what they had quarrelled about. It must have been festering for some long time, because Paul had heard about it in faraway Rome, and he was so concerned that he found it necessary to mention it in his letter, and actually to name the two ladies.[1]

We do not need to be told how unpleasantly close to home Paul's words are. Fractures in the fellowship are all too common, leading someone to write:

> To live above
> With the saints we love;
> Oh, that will be glory!
> But to live below
> With the saints we know;
> Now that's a different story!

Nothing so hinders the cause of Christ as Christians who have unresolved disagreements with each other. Unbelievers are ever eager to pounce on dissension in the church as proof that there is nothing to Christianity. While the church has to work very diligently to publicize the gospel, a church quarrel always publicizes itself. It has winged feet! Let there be a quarrel one evening in a church business meeting, and it will be the talk in the coffee shops the next morning.

> '... that you love one another; as I have loved you, that you also love one another...

We must, therefore, remember the words of the Lord Jesus: 'A new commandment I give to you, that you love one another; as I have loved you, that you also love one another. By this all will know that you are my disciples, if you have love for one another' (John 13:34–35).

And we must ever be slow to take offence and always eager to forgive (James 1:19–21; Eph. 4:31–32).

To the 'true companion' (v. 3)

There is considerable debate about the person the apostle addresses in this verse. Some suggest that the words translated 'true companion' are actually the name 'Syzygus.' Other suggestions are Timothy, Epaphroditus and Lydia.

The identity of the person is not important. He or she, a person who had laboured faithfully with Paul and others, obviously had the respect of all the church members and could, therefore, truly assist Euodia and Syntyche in resolving their quarrel.

Paul's instructions to this person make it clear that quarrels among believers are not to be left to fester but rather are to be quickly dealt with in a spirit of love.

General instructions (vv. 4–9)

Having addressed individuals in the church, Paul now turns to give instructions to all the members.

Rejoice in the Lord (v. 4)

This joy-intoxicated man could not stress too much the importance of his fellow-believers rejoicing, but, as always, the cause of the Christian's rejoicing is the Lord. Paul is not calling here for some kind of general, happy optimism that has no basis. There are no reasons for rejoicing without the Lord, but with him there is no end to such reasons.

Paul's formula for joy is apparent in this letter. We can summarize it by saying we must have:

- **THE CAUSE OF CHRIST** as our priority. That cause, of course, includes the fellowship, the furtherance and the faith of the gospel (1:5,12,27);
- **THE CHARACTER OF CHRIST** as our pattern. This is the character of sacrificially giving one's self up in the interest of others (2:5–8);
- **THE COMPREHENSION OF CHRIST** as our passion. This means crying out with Paul 'that I may know Him' (3:10);
- **THE CARE OF CHRIST** as our peace, which the apostle is about to express (4:6–7).

Those who put these items on their personal agenda and seriously pursue them will find that Paul has indeed given a foolproof formula for joy. They will not have to seek it because it will have sought and found them.

Be gentle (v. 5)

This spirit of being gracious and kind and being willing to put up gently with all that is unpleasant in others is to be demonstrated in their dealing with 'all men'. They would find motivation for doing this by remembering that 'the Lord is at hand,' either near enough to observe their dealings or coming soon to receive from them an accounting.

Trust and pray (vv. 6–7)

Christians are not to be filled with anxiety and tossed with care. They are rather to bring their problems and needs to the Lord with the confidence that he cares for them and his care is sufficient. They are to do so with thanksgiving, remembering how very gracious God has been to them. An ungrateful child always seeks more from his parents without giving thanks for what he has received. We are not to be ungrateful children.

Believers who carry their burdens to the Lord will find peace and rest in their spirits. This peace will stand at the door and guard the hearts and minds of believers so that anxious care and worry cannot enter. It is a glorious peace from the Lord that unbelievers cannot find and cannot explain, and it is a peace that believers themselves cannot fully understand.

Think about the right things (v. 8)

The book of Proverbs says: '… as he thinks in his heart, so is he' (Prov. 23:7).

In keeping with that thought, Paul suggests to his readers a 'divine programming' that will ensure their peace. He calls upon them to think about:

- **THE TRUE**—those things that correspond to the teaching of God's Word;
- **THE NOBLE**—those things that have the dignity of moral excellence;
- **THE JUST**—those things that conform to God's standards;
- **THE PURE**—those things that are free from the taint of sin;
- **THE LOVELY**—those virtues that make believers attractive and winsome, such as generosity, kindness, compassion and willingness to forgive;
- **THE THINGS OF GOOD REPORT**—those things that give Christians a good reputation and a good name.

Paul sums it all up by telling his readers to meditate on anything of virtue and anything worthy of praise.

Paul concludes this set of instructions to the church with these words: 'The things which you learned and received and heard and saw in me, these do, and the God of peace will be with you' (v. 9).

> Every pastor is called to set the kind of example that others can follow

This is the third time that Paul has explicitly called his readers to follow his example (2:17–18; 3:17). It must be said again that Paul is not merely giving way here to pride. Every pastor is called to set the kind of example that others can follow. If one is doing this, he can safely call others to follow him.

For further study ▶

FOR FURTHER STUDY

1. Read the following Scriptures: Psalm 133:1; Romans 12:16; 14:19; 15:5; 1 Corinthians 1:10; 2 Corinthians 13:11; Ephesians 4:3; 1 Peter 3:8. How important is it for believers in Christ to maintain unity? What can be done to promote improved relationships?
2. Paul urges his readers to let their gentleness be known. Read Matthew 11:28–30; 12:15–21. To whom do these verses refer?
3. Paul also exhorts the Philippians to not be anxious. Read Matthew 6:19–34. What truths can you identify as being vital for ridding ourselves of anxiety?

TO THINK ABOUT AND DISCUSS

1. It is easy to allow discord and petty rivalry to enter into our relationships. Identify areas in which you know this is presently taking place. How may the principles outlined and explained in this section bring correction and healing in these strained relationships?
2. Some people consider joy merely a feeling to be experienced. How does the teaching in this section put joy into the clearer perspective of living a life in close relationship with the Lord Jesus Christ? What other practical elements are involved in the cultivation of joy?
3. For personal and private consideration: Paul could call other believers to follow his own example as a follower of Christ. What specific areas of your life do you think you need to work on if, in following your example, others are not to fall into some of your sinful habits?

10 A closing testimony

(4:10–20)

After stressing these things, the apostle shifts his attention and expresses personal gratitude for the caring ministry of the Philippians (4:10,16–18)

Paul expresses gratitude for a gift from the Philippians (vv. 10, 14–18)

Thanksgiving overflowed easily from the apostle Paul, whether to God for his innumerable blessings or to others for their friendship and kindness.

In these verses, it is the latter. William Hendriksen explains:

> As soon as the news of Paul's imprisonment had become known in Philippi the desire had sprung up 'to do something' to help him. But at first no favorable opportunity had presented itself. It may have been that no messenger had been immediately available, or that for some reason or other it had been impossible to collect the gift from the various members. These are only two out of many possibilities. At any rate, for

a while opportunity to send the gift had been lacking. As soon as this situation changed, the Philippians had acted with characteristic enthusiasm and devotion.[1]

Paul had come to expect this kind of support from this generous church. When other churches failed to give (v. 15), this church had 'sent aid once and again' (v. 16).

All of this was reason for Paul to engage in exuberant rejoicing. The Philippians had generously given, but Paul 'rejoiced in the Lord greatly' (v. 10), knowing that the Lord had worked in them (2:13).

While Paul certainly admitted that he had benefited from their gift, he wanted his readers to know that there were other benefits as well:

- **THEIR GIFT WOULD ABOUND TO THEIR ACCOUNT (V. 17).** Everything Christians do for the kingdom of God is an investment that repays rich dividends. Hendriksen notes: 'Among the fruits that are harvested by such givers may be mentioned the following: a good conscience, assurance of salvation, enriched fellowship with other believers, a broadened outlook into the needs and interests of the church universal, increased joy and love … a higher degree of glory in heaven, Judgment Day praise.'[2]
- **THEIR GIFT BROUGHT PLEASURE TO GOD,** who looked upon them as fragrant offerings (v. 19).

Paul expresses contentment in his circumstances (vv. 11–13)

While Paul was grateful for the gift of the Philippians, he did not want them to think that he was one who went about with his hand out. Paul was thankful for the gift, but he was supremely thankful that the Lord had taught him to be content in every circumstance (vv. 11–12).

What was the key to Paul's contentment? He answers: 'I can do all things through Christ who strengthens me' (v. 13).

This was not something that slipped from Paul's pen in an unguarded moment in which he was caught up with emotion. He genuinely experienced the strength of Christ. When he pleaded with the Lord to remove a physical condition from him, the Lord responded: 'My grace is sufficient for you, for my strength is made perfect in weakness' (2 Cor. 12:9–10).

He would later write, when completely forsaken by others, 'But the Lord stood with me and strengthened me…' (2 Tim. 4:17).

Although God's people are called to be diligent in ministering to their brothers and sisters in Christ, they sometimes fail. When others fail us, we should be glad that the Lord never fails. And when we do not receive ministry from others, we should content ourselves with God and his sufficiency.

When others fail us, we should be glad that the Lord never fails

The best loved of all the psalms begins:

> The LORD is my shepherd; I shall not want (Ps. 23:1).

With the Lord as his shepherd, the psalmist (probably David) knew he would not lack anything he truly needed.

The prophet Habakkuk discovered the same truth. He put it like this:

> Though the fig tree may not blossom,
> Nor fruit be on the vines;

> Though the labour of the olive may fail,
> And the fields yield no food;
> Though the flock may be cut off from the fold,
> And there be no herd in the stalls—
> Yet I will rejoice in the LORD,
> I will joy in the God of my salvation.
> The LORD God is my strength;
> He will make my feet like deer's feet,
> And he will make me walk on my high hills
> (Hab. 3:17–19).

While we certainly do not consider ourselves to have attained the spiritual level of Paul, David or Habakkuk, the marvellous truth is that we, too, can draw strength from the Lord, as verse 19 indicates.

Paul expresses an assurance (v. 19)

This verse has often been misunderstood. It does not tell us that God's people will never experience or feel a need. It rather tells us that God will supply the needs of his people. He sometimes does this by meeting the need and sometimes by giving his people the strength to face the need, as the apostle has already testified (v. 13).

Israel's great king David says to the Lord:

> For by you I can run against a troop.
> And by my God I can leap over a wall.
> (Ps. 18:29).

We prefer always to leap over the wall of need, leaving it

behind. But we should not despise the other possibility—that is, God enabling us to run against or go through a troop. Sometimes God takes us right through the need, giving us strength as we go. David himself experienced this on several occasions, most notably when he went out to meet the giant Goliath. God could have removed Goliath, causing him to vaporize as David approached. Instead God gave David the strength to face and to defeat him.

Needs that simply get vaporized may seem more glamorous, but strength to face and meet needs is just as much from God.

Paul expresses a prayer (v. 20)

We should not dismiss these words as mere formality. Yes, Paul is bringing his letter to a close, but he means every word of this verse. It is his fervent desire to see God receive glory and honour both in this life and in the life to come.

God is worthy of honour because he is God. He is the sovereign creator and ruler of all things. He is clothed in majesty and splendour beyond our ability to comprehend. He is eternal, holy, faithful, just and true. He is unlimited in wisdom and power. He is immeasurably kind and gracious.

God is also worthy of honour because he is Father. He is the Father of all those whom by grace he has adopted into his family (Rom. 8:14–17; Gal. 4:5; Eph. 1:5). As their Father, he loves them with an undying love and tenderly supplies their needs and protects them from any real harm.

Such a God deserves our praise and worship both in this life and in the life to come. Eternity itself will not be sufficient to praise him adequately. As Paul pondered the greatness and glory of God and the worship of the saints in eternity, he could not help but say 'Amen,' that is, 'Let it be.' May we add our own 'Amen' to his.

FOR FURTHER STUDY

1. Read 2 Corinthians 8:1–15. Who does Paul use as examples of giving? Read 2 Corinthians 9:6–15. How are Christians to give? What are the results of generous giving for those who give and for those who receive?
2. Read 1 Timothy 6:6–10. What does Paul consider to be 'great gain'? What destroys contentment? Read Psalm 145 for an example of contentment.

TO THINK ABOUT AND DISCUSS

1. Some people consider financial prosperity to be the right of a child of God. How does the experience of the apostle Paul bring a different perspective to this kind of thinking?
2. The church has a responsibility to ensure that its ministers and missionaries are adequately financially rewarded for their labours. What steps do you consider church officers and other leaders in the church should possibly take in the light of this passage?

Conclusion

(4:21–23)

The final words of Paul's letter abound with tenderness and affection. He essentially says: 'Give my love to every member of the church. All the people here send their love to you'

As we have noticed, Paul was able to refer to the saints in Caesar's household because God had used the apostle's imprisonment to further the gospel (1:12–13). Paul was living proof that children of God can be true and faithful even in difficult circumstances and hostile environments. Even a citadel of Satan can become a centre for the gospel.

In some cultures it is customary when meeting a friend to point in succession to the heart, the lips and the forehead. This greeting says: 'My heart loves you, my lips speak well of you and my mind thinks the best of you.'

Paul undoubtedly felt the same toward the Philippians. Each Christian should be able to say in heartfelt fashion the same to other believers.

End notes

Background and Summary

1 **Roger Ellsworth,** *The Guide: The Bible Book by Book,* Evangelical Press, pp. 334-5.

Chapter 1—
Paul introduces his letter

1 **Howard F. Vos,** *Bible Study Commentary: Philippians*, Zondervan Publishing House, p. 31.

2 **William Hendriksen,** *New Testament Commentary: Exposition of Philippians*, Baker Book House, pp.61-2.

Chapter 2—
Paul rejoices in his imprisonment

1 **Hendriksen,** *Philippians*, pp. 71-2.

2 Cited in **J.I. Packer** *Knowing God*, InterVarsity Press, p.27.

3 **Richard Sibbes,** *Works of Richard Sibbes*, The Banner of Truth Trust, vol. i, p. 340.

Chapter 3—
Urgent appeals

1 **Warren Wiersbe,** *The Bible Exposition Commentary*, Victor Books, vol. ii, p. 70.

2 **Matthew Henry,** *Matthew Henry's Commentary*, Fleming H. Revell Publishing Company, vol. vi, p. 730.

3 **Hendriksen,** *Philippians*, p. 99.

4 As above, p.108.

5 **Charles Wesley** *And can it be*

Chapter 4—
Applying the mind of Christ

1 **Alec Motyer,** *The Bible Speaks Today: The Message of Philippians*, Inter-Varsity Press, p.135.

2 As above.

Chapter 5—
The mind of Christ exemplified

1 **Michael Bentley,** *Shining in the Darkness*, Evangelical Press, p. 91.

2 **Wiersbe,** *The Bible Exposition Commentary*, vol. ii, p.81.

Chapter 6—
A warning about confidence in the flesh

1 **Bentley,** *Shining in the Darkness,* p.105.
2 **Hendriksen,** *Philippians,* p.153.
3 As above.
4 **Fanny J. Crosby,** *Saved by grace*

Chapter 7—
Passionately pursuing

1 **Johnson Oatman, Jr,** (1856-1922), *Higher Ground*
2 **Marvin R. Vincent,** *Word Studies in the New Testament,* vol. iii, p. 451 William B. Eerdmans Publishing Company

Chapter 9—
Important instructions

1 **Bentley,** *Shining in the Darkness,* p.145.

Chapter 10—A closing testimony

1 **Hendriksen,** *Philippians,* p.204.
2 As above, p. 208.

Additional resources

James Montgomery Boice, *Philippians: An Expositional Commentary*, Baker Book House

John Gill, *Exposition of the Old & New Testaments*, vol. ix, The Baptist Standard Bearer

D. Martyn Lloyd-Jones, *The Life of Joy: An Exposition of Philippians 1 and 2*, Baker Book House

D. Martyn Lloyd-Jones, *The Life of Peace: An Exposition of Philippians 3 and 4*, Baker Book House

John MacArthur, *The MacArthur New Testament Commentary: Philippians*, Moody Publications

Richard R. Melick, Jr., *The New American Commentary*, vol xxxii, Broadman Press.